WHAT'S GOOD FOR YOU?

WELCOME TO
WHAT'S GOOD FOR YOU?
GOOD LUCK!

WHICH ONE IS GOOD FOR YOU?

ORANGES
ARE GOOD FOR YOU!

VEGETABLES ARE GOOD FOR YOU
CAN YOU SPOT ALL FIVE?

THESE ARE THE 5 HEALTHY VEGETABLES!

EXERCISE IS GOOD FOR YOU
WHICH OF THESE ISN'T AN EXERCISE?

SITTING DOWN
ISN'T AN
EXERCISE!

UNHEALTHY FOOD
WHICH IS THE ODD ONE OUT?

TOMATO
IS THE
ODD ONE OUT!

WHICH MEAL IS GOOD FOR YOU?

THIS MEAL IS GOOD FOR YOU!

SPORTS ARE **GOOD FOR YOU**
HOW MANY CAN YOU SPOT HERE?

boxing

THERE ARE 6 SPORTS HERE!

swimming   baseball

basketball

tennis

skateboarding

HEALTHY FRUIT AND VEGETABLES?
CAN YOU SPOT ALL FIVE?

THESE ARE THE 5 HEALTHY FRUIT & VEGETABLES!

HEALTHY FOOD & DRINK
WHO HAS THE MOST?

THE GIRL HAS THE MOST HEALTHY FOOD & DRINK!

EXERCISE IS **GOOD FOR YOU**
HOW MANY KIDS ARE EXERCISING HERE?

ONLY TWO KIDS ARE EXERCISING HERE!

DO YOU KNOW YOUR FRUITS?
WHICH TWO ARE WRONG?

CHERRY

LEMON

ORANGE

APPLE

APRICOT

STRAWBERRY

WATERMELON

PEAR

PINEAPPLE

THIS ISN'T
A PEAR...

IT'S A
STRAWBERRY!

THIS ISN'T
A STRAWBERRY...

IT'S
A PEAR!

WHICH ONE IS GOOD FOR YOU?

APPLES

ARE GOOD
FOR YOU!

EXERCISE TOYS
WHO HAS THE MOST?

THE BOY HAS THE MOST EXERCISE TOYS!

WHERE'S THE FRUIT AND VEGETABLES?
CAN YOU SPOT ALL FIVE?

THESE ARE THE 5 HEALTHY FRUIT & VEGETABLES!

WHAT'S HEALTHY?
CAN YOU SPOT ALL FOUR?

THESE ARE THE 4 HEALTHY ITEMS!

EXERCISE IS **GOOD FOR YOU**
HOW MANY CAN YOU SPOT HERE?

THERE ARE 5 EXERCISES HERE!

HEALTHY FRUIT AND VEGETABLES
WHICH IS THE ODD ONE OUT?

LOLLIPOPS

ARE THE
ODD ONE OUT!

FRUITS ARE GOOD FOR YOU
CAN YOU SPOT ALL FIVE?

THESE ARE THE 5 HEALTHY FRUITS!

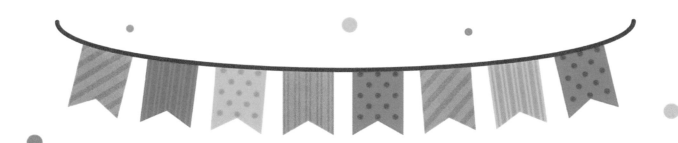

THE END!

Find us on Amazon!

Discover all of the titles available in our store;
including these below...

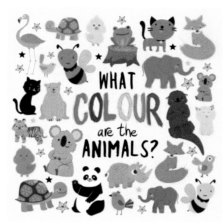

Made in the USA
Columbia, SC
15 July 2019